Savvy

MORE MEAT PLEASE!

DELICIOUS
SANDWICHES

for
Meat-Eating
KIDS

written by
ALISON DEERING

illustrated by
BOB LENTZ

CAPSTONE PRESS
a capstone imprint

TO MY DAD, WHO TAUGHT ME THE BEAUTY OF A GREAT LUNCH SANDWICH, AND TO MY MOM, WHO STILL MAKES ME SANDWICHES NOW. — AD

TO THE SAUCEMAN. SORRY THERE ISN'T MORE RANCH DRESSING IN HERE. — BL

Savvy Books are published by Capstone Press,
1710 Roe Crest Drive, North Mankato, Minnesota 56003
www.mycapstone.com

Library of Congress Cataloging-in-Publication Data

Names: Deering, Alison, author.
Title: More meat please! : delicious sandwiches for meat-eating kids / by Alison Deering.
Description: North Mankato, Minnesota : Capstone Press, [2017] | Series:
  Savvy. Between the bread | Audience: Age 9–13. | Audience: Grade 4–6. | Includes bibliographical references and index.
Identifiers: LCCN 2017008313 | ISBN 9781515739210 (hardcover)
Subjects: LCSH: Sandwiches—Juvenile literature. | LCGFT: Cookbooks.
Classification: LCC TX818 .D45 2017 | DDC 641.84—dc23
LC record available at https://lccn.loc.gov/2017008313

Designer: Bob Lentz
Creative Director: Heather Kindseth
Production Specialist: Tori Abraham

Printed in the United States of America.
010373F17

TABLE OF CONTENTS

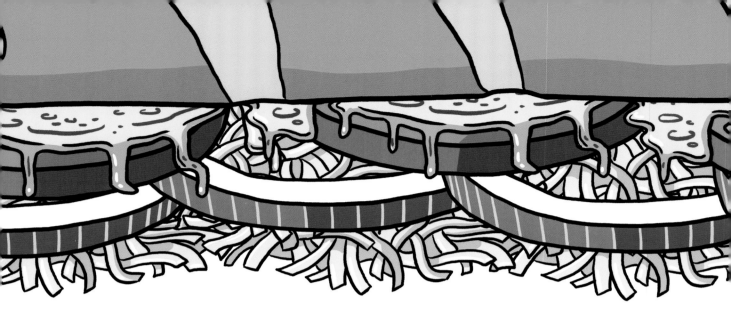

INTRODUCTION

(AKA WHAT IS A SANDWICH)

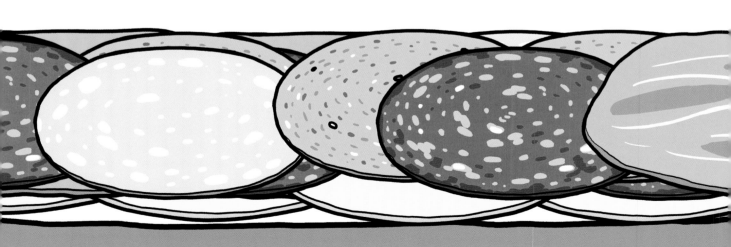

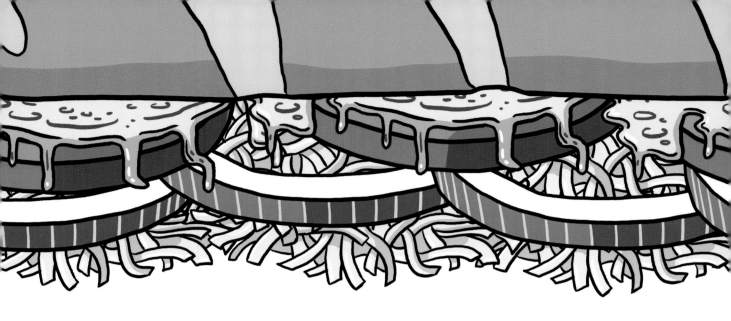

What makes a sandwich a sandwich? According to the United States Department of Agriculture, the "Product must contain at least 35 percent cooked meat and no more than 50 percent bread." The dictionary is slightly more open-minded, describing a sandwich as "two or more slices of bread or a split roll having a filling in between."

But what about wraps? What about open-face sandwiches? What about un-wiches? That's why, for our purposes, a sandwich is whatever you make of it! Wrap it, fold it, stack it, slice it — you be the judge when it comes to your meaty masterpiece. Just keep in mind that no matter what, a great sandwich starts with the basics — the ingredients. Meat, cheese, and toppings can make or break a sandwich, so choose wisely and have fun!

The beauty and genius of a delicious sandwich is that YOU as the chef and creator can make it anything you want it to be. And with this guidebook to what happens between the bread, you'll learn how to build the best sandwiches ever.

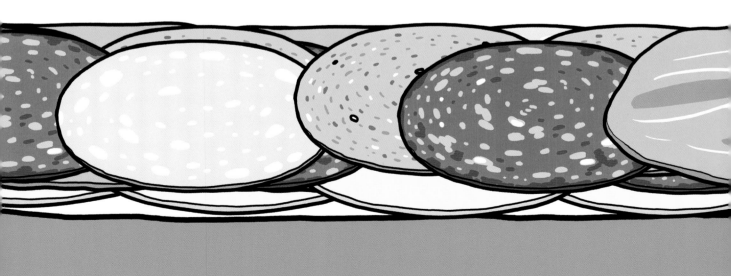

BOLOGNA*

Whether you spell it "bologna" or "baloney," this sandwich has been a must-have in American lunchboxes for years, especially in the Midwest and South. Keep it simple, keep it basic. That's the beauty of bologna. Fussing it up with anything else is just . . . well, a bunch of baloney.

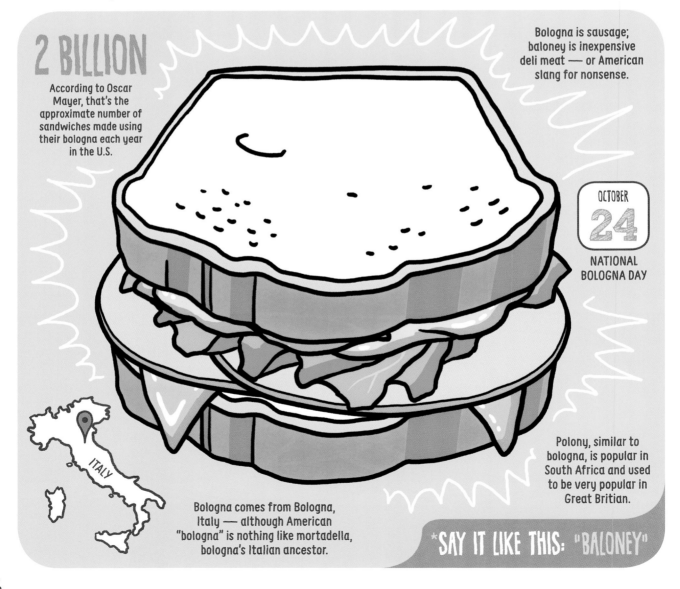

2 BILLION

According to Oscar Mayer, that's the approximate number of sandwiches made using their bologna each year in the U.S.

Bologna is sausage; baloney is inexpensive deli meat — or American slang for nonsense.

OCTOBER 24

NATIONAL BOLOGNA DAY

ITALY

Bologna comes from Bologna, Italy — although American "bologna" is nothing like mortadella, bologna's Italian ancestor.

Polony, similar to bologna, is popular in South Africa and used to be very popular in Great Britian.

*SAY IT LIKE THIS: "BALONEY"

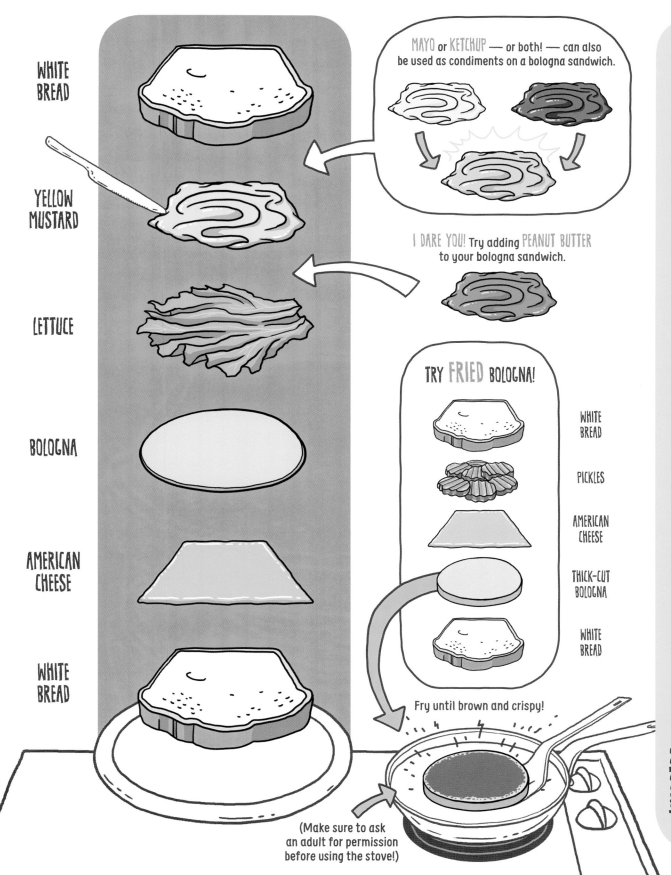

WHITE BREAD

YELLOW MUSTARD

LETTUCE

BOLOGNA

AMERICAN CHEESE

WHITE BREAD

MAYO or KETCHUP — or both! — can also be used as condiments on a bologna sandwich.

I DARE YOU! Try adding PEANUT BUTTER to your bologna sandwich.

TRY FRIED BOLOGNA!

WHITE BREAD

PICKLES

AMERICAN CHEESE

THICK-CUT BOLOGNA

WHITE BREAD

Fry until brown and crispy!

(Make sure to ask an adult for permission before using the stove!)

HAM AND CHEESE

A ham and cheese sandwich is a classic, and the best part is, it's completely customizable! This version is made with cheddar, but any cheese will do — mozzarella, Swiss, American, you name it! You can also add as many toppings as you'd like. Start with lettuce, tomato, and onion, then add mayo, mustard, or both! If you're feeling fancy, try grilling your sandwich. Just make sure to ask a grownup for help and permission before using the stove.

288 FT.
The longest ham and cheese sandwich ever created, made by 70 students and staff in Singapore.

#2
A basic ham sandwich is the second most popular sandwich in America.

A *croque monsieur* is the French version of a grilled ham and cheese sandwich.

In the United Kingdom, it's common to add pickles to ham and cheese sandwiches.

130.9 FT.
The world's longest ham sandwich, created in Spain in 2009.

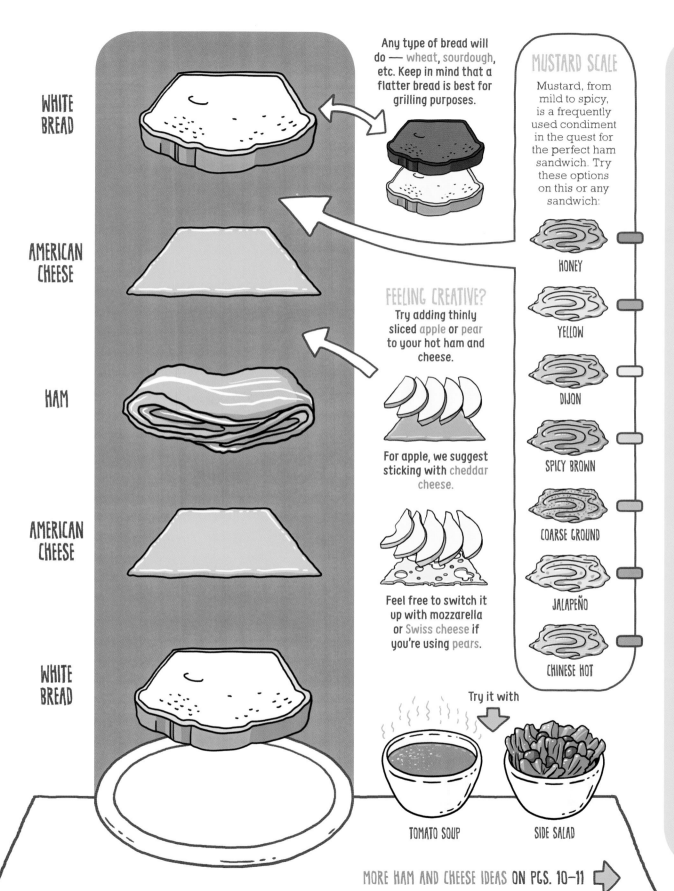

WHITE BREAD

AMERICAN CHEESE

HAM

AMERICAN CHEESE

WHITE BREAD

Any type of bread will do — wheat, sourdough, etc. Keep in mind that a flatter bread is best for grilling purposes.

FEELING CREATIVE?

Try adding thinly sliced apple or pear to your hot ham and cheese.

For apple, we suggest sticking with cheddar cheese.

Feel free to switch it up with mozzarella or Swiss cheese if you're using pears.

MUSTARD SCALE

Mustard, from mild to spicy, is a frequently used condiment in the quest for the perfect ham sandwich. Try these options on this or any sandwich:

HONEY

YELLOW

DIJON

SPICY BROWN

COARSE GROUND

JALAPEÑO

CHINESE HOT

Try it with

TOMATO SOUP

SIDE SALAD

MORE HAM AND CHEESE IDEAS ON PGS. 10–11

HAM AND CHEESE

BETWEEN THE BREAD:

THE HISTORY OF THE HAM AND CHEESE

Sandwiches may be traceable all the way back to ancient times, but what type of sandwich claims the title of coming first? We may not know the specifics, but what we DO know is that the ham sandwich is one of the earliest known closed-face sandwiches. By 1850, London street vendors were selling it, and by 1894, the ham and cheese sandwich had made the jump to America. The sandwich was even sold at baseball games — along with ice cream and lemonade — at one time. (Hot dogs were introduced later.)

But who's really responsible? According to the *Larousse Gastronomique 1961*, that would be Patrick Connolly, an eighteenth-century Irish immigrant to England. Connolly paired ham, Leicester cheese, and some type of mayo on a roll and started selling it. In some areas this might still be called "a Connolly."

Not one to let the Brits get a jump on them, the French likely started pairing ham and cheese on bread around the same time period. But it wasn't until the 20th century that they gifted us with their toasty version, the croque monsieur.

The ham and cheese has a lot to offer beyond being a basic, classic sandwich. You can also serve your ham and cheese hot — in fact, we recommend it! Just fire up your stove, butter the outsides of the bread, and grill it up until the outsides are crispy and the insides are melty. If you have a panini press you can also make your hot ham and cheese that way.

WE DARE YOU!

Ham and cheese is great on its own, but a sandwich savant like you is probably ready to take it to the next level. Think you can handle the weird, the gross, the amazing, and everything in between? Here are just a few out-there options to experiment with . . . if you dare!

CHOCOLATE

ICE CREAM

HONEY

CHEESE PUFFS

JELLY

PEANUT BUTTER

POTATO CHIPS

BANANAS

APPLE PIE FILLING

SAUERKRAUT

ROAST BEEF

A classic, comforting treat, the roast beef sandwich has been a Boston-area specialty since the 1950s. But it's been in existence long before that. Roast beef goes all the way back to jolly old England, where it's been eaten for at least two centuries. (It's the nation's signature dish.) And who can blame them? An easy-to-customize roast beef sandwich, like this beef and cheddar version, is something you want to take credit for.

1877

A recipe for "Beefsteak Toast" — an early version of the roast beef sandwich — is published.

What's in a name? Arby's actually stands for R.B., the initials of the Raffel brothers — and coincidentally, roast beef.

1951

Kelly's Roast Beef, a Boston-area restaurant, claims to have invented the roast beef sandwich this year.

Roast beef sandwiches can be eaten hot or cold!

1964

Arby's was founded, taking the roast beef sandwich mainstream — or at least making it fast food.

Why roast beef? The Raffel brothers, the founders of Arby's, were inspired by a $0.79 roast beef sandwich, which they found at a Boston-area sandwich shop one rainy Halloween night.

HAMBURGER BUN

CHEDDAR CHEESE

ROAST BEEF

HAMBURGER BUN

OTHER ROAST BEEF VARIATIONS:

CORNED BEEF

PASTRAMI

FRENCH DIP
(See pg. 40)

HORSERADISH SAUCE

GRILLED ONIONS

TOMATO

LETTUCE

PROVOLONE CHEESE

SWISS CHEESE

BEEF ON WECK

Typically found in western New York, the beef on weck is a regional take on the traditional roast beef sandwich. This version is made with rare, thinly sliced roast beef and horseradish piled on a kummelweck roll — a kaiser roll topped with pretzel salt and caraway seeds.

Serve with a side of leftover mashed potatoes or french fries.

Open up the sandwich and drop the leftover mashed and gravy on top to make a hot beef commercial!

MUFFULETTA*

Make way for the muffuletta! This regional sandwich got its start in the Big Easy, aka New Orleans, Louisiana, and remains a specialty there to this day. Interestingly enough, despite the muffuletta having a decidedly Italian background, the sandwich is nowhere to be found in Italy. So how do you eat it? A muffuletta is typically served at room temperature, and while some may protest, we say there's nothing wrong with toasting yours up if the mood strikes.

The sandwich was not always called a muffuletta — the name carried over from the muffuletto bread the sandwich was made on.

LATE 1800S–EARLY 1900S

The muffuletta is the brainchild of Sicilian immigrants, who arrived and settled in New Orleans.

LA

1906

The first muffuletta sandwich was made by Salvatore Lupo at Central Grocery, his specialty market in New Orleans's French Quarter.

10"

The approximate diameter of a loaf of muffuletta bread.

*SAY IT LIKE THIS: "MOO-FU-LEHT-UH"

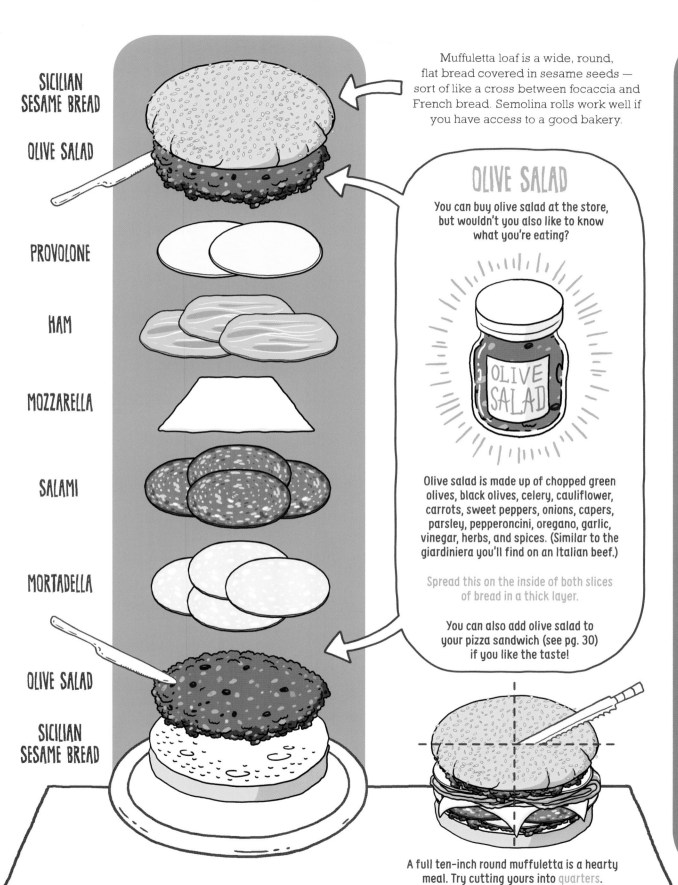

SICILIAN SESAME BREAD

OLIVE SALAD

PROVOLONE

HAM

MOZZARELLA

SALAMI

MORTADELLA

OLIVE SALAD

SICILIAN SESAME BREAD

Muffuletta loaf is a wide, round, flat bread covered in sesame seeds — sort of like a cross between focaccia and French bread. Semolina rolls work well if you have access to a good bakery.

OLIVE SALAD

You can buy olive salad at the store, but wouldn't you also like to know what you're eating?

Olive salad is made up of chopped green olives, black olives, celery, cauliflower, carrots, sweet peppers, onions, capers, parsley, pepperoncini, oregano, garlic, vinegar, herbs, and spices. (Similar to the giardiniera you'll find on an Italian beef.)

Spread this on the inside of both slices of bread in a thick layer.

You can also add olive salad to your pizza sandwich (see pg. 30) if you like the taste!

A full ten-inch round muffuletta is a hearty meal. Try cutting yours into quarters.

MUFFULETTA

CLASSIC ITALIAN

A classic Italian sub sandwich is practically an art form, and what's even more beautiful is that this sandwich is just as good at home as it is at an old-school Italian deli. Picture cold cuts piled high on a hoagie roll, topped with lettuce, tomato, and onion, and drizzled with oil and vinegar. The hardest part about enjoying this sandwich just might be fitting it in your mouth.

500 The number of "hero sandwiches" said to have been ordered by a local Navy submarine base in New London, Connecticut during WWII. Rumor has it that the deli workers started referring to the hero as a "sub" and the name stuck!

LATE-19TH TO MID-20TH CENTURY It was during this period that the Italian sandwich started popping up in Italian-American communities in the northeastern United States.

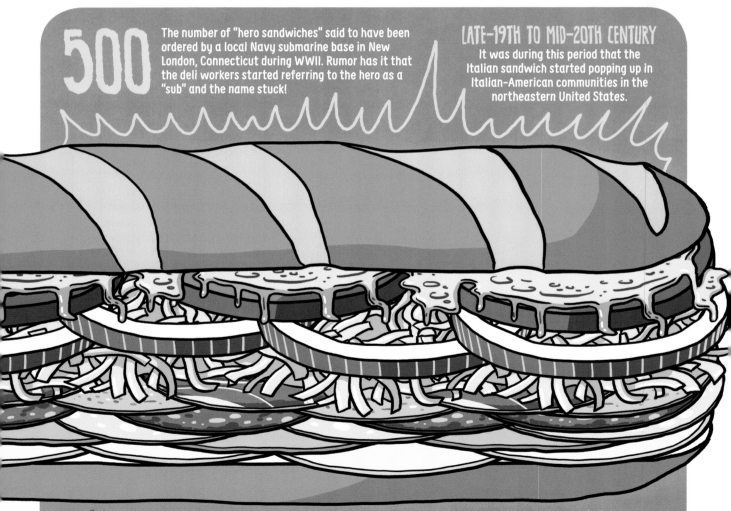

ME Portland, Maine, claims to be the birthplace of the Italian sandwich — it's the state's signature sammie.

1902 The year Giovanni Amato, a baker, invented the Italian sandwich in Portland, Maine.

1965 The first Subway sandwich shop opened.

ITALIAN-STYLE HOAGIE

OIL & VINEGAR

TOMATOES

ONIONS

SHREDDED ICEBERG LETTUCE

CAPICOLA

COTTO SALAMI

SALAMI

MORTADELLA

HAM

PROVOLONE CHEESE

ITALIAN-STYLE HOAGIE

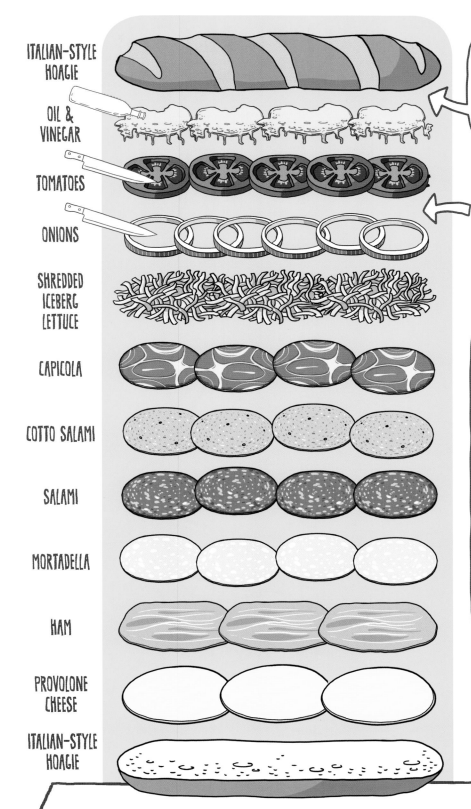

PRO TIP!

Bookend your Italian sub with an extra pieces of cheese on top to keep the bread from getting soggy.

You can also add hot peppers to your classic Italian sub if you like things a little spicy.

Or try sweet peppers for a milder taste.

WHAT'S IN A NAME?

The classic Italian has more than a dozen regional identifiers in the U.S. A submarine sandwich is most common, but which one do you use?

HOAGIE	Philadelphia
HERO	New York
GRINDER	New England
BLIMPIE	New Jersey
ZEPPELIN	Eastern Pennsylvania
TORPEDO	New York or New Jersey
WEDGE	Upstate New York
GATSBY	Cape Town, South Africa

Try it with

POTATO CHIPS

COLA

BLT (BACON, LETTUCE, TOMATO)

Nothing says summer like a BLT. Farm-fresh tomatoes pair perfectly with crispy, greasy bacon and cool, refreshing lettuce. And the best part is, a BLT is a sandwich best enjoyed at home. Just toast your bread, pile on your ingredients, and pull up a seat — preferably at an outdoor table — to enjoy!

#7
The BLT is the seventh most popular sandwich in the U.S. according to a 2014 survey.

The abbreviation BLT likely started in American diners and restaurants before it caught on with the general public.

1,980 LBS.
The weight of the world's longest BLT.

APRIL
NATIONAL BLT MONTH

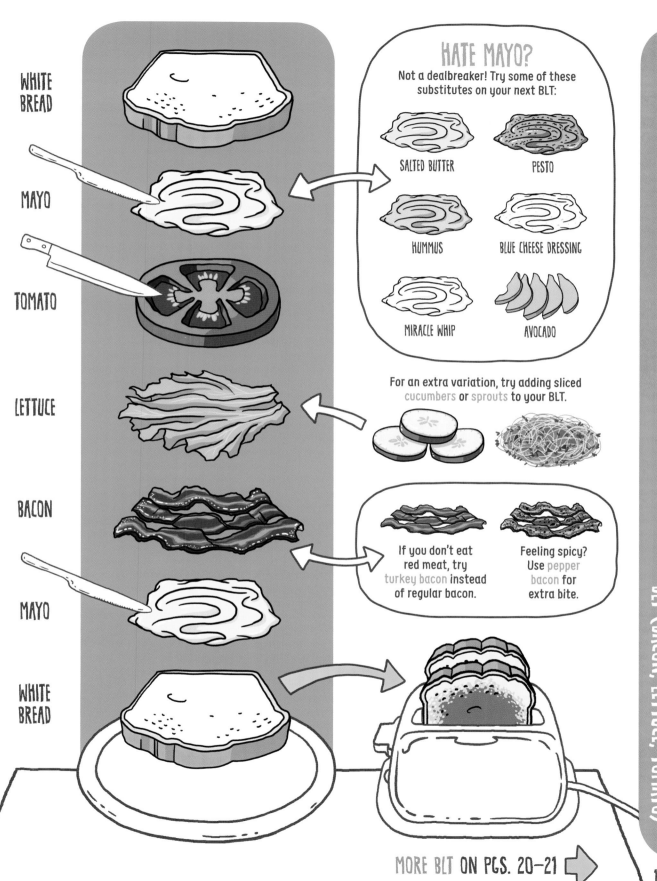

WHITE BREAD

MAYO

TOMATO

LETTUCE

BACON

MAYO

WHITE BREAD

HATE MAYO?

Not a dealbreaker! Try some of these substitutes on your next BLT:

SALTED BUTTER

PESTO

HUMMUS

BLUE CHEESE DRESSING

MIRACLE WHIP

AVOCADO

For an extra variation, try adding sliced cucumbers or sprouts to your BLT.

If you don't eat red meat, try turkey bacon instead of regular bacon.

Feeling spicy? Use pepper bacon for extra bite.

MORE BLT ON PGS. 20–21

BLT (BACON, LETTUCE, TOMATO)

THE HISTORY OF THE BLT

Given all the casual, delicious glory that goes along with BLTs, you might be surprised to learn that they did not actually start out as a casual sandwich. In fact, BLTs are actually a distant descendant of Victorian-era tea sandwiches. (And you can't get much fancier than a Victorian-era tearoom!) Many of the facts behind the rise of the BLT — including when the abbreviation first came into use — aren't set in stone. As is the case with many great recipes, this is one that evolved over time.

But there are a few things we know to be true:

16TH CEN.	Tomatoes are introduced to Europe.
18TH CEN.	Mayonnaise is invented in France.
1903	*Good Housekeeping Everyday Cook Book* publishes a recipe for a club sandwich, which included bacon, lettuce, and tomato, along with mayo and a slice of turkey. (One of the earliest mentions of something resembling a BLT.)
1940s	BLTs become popular following WWII thanks to the rise of supermarkets, meaning fresh tomatoes and lettuce are available year round.
1958	Hellman's Mayonnaise advertises their product as "traditional on bacon, lettuce, and tomato sandwiches."
2011	The world's largest BLT is created during Iron Barley's seventh annual Tomato Fest in St. Louis, Missouri. It was 224 feet long and 18 inches wide and contained 600 pounds of bacon, 550 pounds of tomatoes, 220 heads of lettuce, and 440 pounds of bread!

WE DARE YOU!

A BLT is great on its own, but a sandwich savant like you is probably ready to take it to the next level. Think you can handle the weird, the gross, the amazing, and everything in between? Here are just a few out-there options to experiment with . . . if you dare!

CHOCOLATE CHIP COOKIE

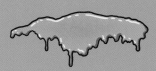
BUFFALO SAUCE

MAC & CHEESE

MARSHMALLOW FLUFF

PEANUT BUTTER

FRIED EGG

FRENCH FRIES

MASHED POTATOES

JALAPEÑOS

RADISHES

21

CLUB

Stack your BLT sky high and toss on some turkey and you've got yourself a club sandwich. This tall sandwich is a real mouthful — layers upon layers of toasty bread, crisp bacon, and savory turkey, plus lettuce, tomato, and mayo stack up to create the classic club. The only limit is how much sandwich you can fit in your mouth in one bite.

1894

The year the club sandwich is rumored to have been created at the Saratoga Club House, a gambling establishment in Saratoga Springs, New York.

The club sandwich has a more formal name too — the clubhouse sandwich.

1903

The first recipe for a club sandwich appears in the *Good Housekeeping Everyday Cook Book.*

Club sandwiches are usually cut into quarters, making them triangle shaped and easier to eat when the sandwich is stacked high!

TOASTED
WHITE BREAD

MAYO

TURKEY

BACON

TOMATO

LETTUCE

MAYO

TOASTED
WHITE BREAD

Make your club sandwich a double-decker delight by adding a third slice of bread. Just repeat the order of ingredients on the second layer.

Technically speaking, a club sandwich can be made with chicken or turkey. The choice of protein is up to you!

MAKE IT YOUR OWN!

Just like the BLT, a club sandwich is easy to customize:

If you don't eat red meat, use turkey bacon instead of regular bacon.

Feeling spicy? Try pepper bacon for extra bite.

Try adding cucumber or avocado.

Sub in wheat bread for white.

(You'll probably also need a long toothpick to hold your creation together.)

Serve with another American classic — fries!

Toast your bread before building this sandwich to keep it from getting soggy!

CLUB

23

SPAGHETTI

Let's face it — some foods are just better the next day. That's the beauty of this delicious — and admittedly messy — spaghetti sandwich. You don't have to worry about whipping up a fresh batch of pasta for this one. Just open the fridge, find those leftover noodles, then add meat sauce, cheese, and garlic bread to create a handheld Italian feast!

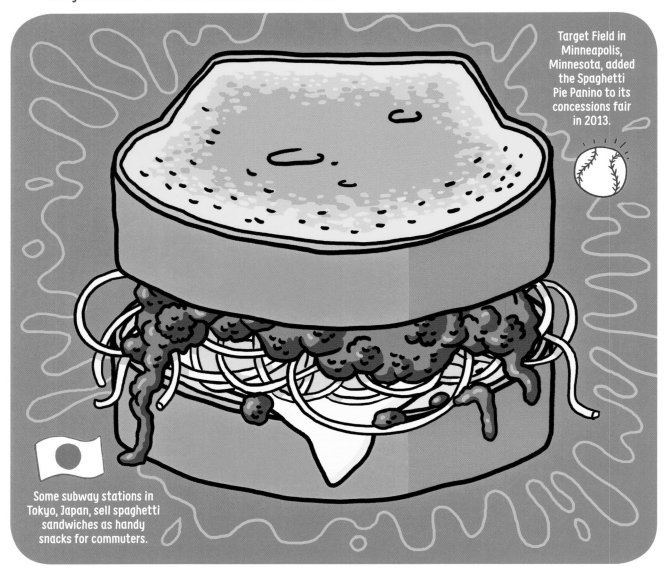

Target Field in Minneapolis, Minnesota, added the Spaghetti Pie Panino to its concessions fair in 2013.

Some subway stations in Tokyo, Japan, sell spaghetti sandwiches as handy snacks for commuters.

OVEN-TOASTED GARLIC BREAD

Don't forget to butter both slices of bread, and feel free to add parmesan, garlic powder, or oregano for extra flavor!

MEAT SAUCE

This spaghetti sandwich uses meat sauce, but you can easily use plain tomato sauce if you prefer.

SPAGHETTI

Swap the tomato sauce for pesto!

MOZZARELLA CHEESE

Leftover spaghetti can be used and eaten hot or cold.

OVEN-TOASTED GARLIC BREAD

Try it on a hot dog bun!

Bake your garlic toast for a few minutes to get it warm, toasty, and crunchy! Make sure to ask an adult for help before using the oven.

BAKE 350° TIMER 10:00

Try it with

SIDE SALAD

SPARKLING WATER

25

MEATBALL SUB

Not sure what to do with those leftover meatballs from dinner? Grab a hoagie roll, some extra cheese, and turn the whole thing into a sandwich, of course! It might be messy, but it'll also be delicious. Pile all your ingredients onto a sliced roll, and ask an adult to help you stick it under the broiler until the cheese is nice and bubbly. Then enjoy eating! You won't need any help for that.

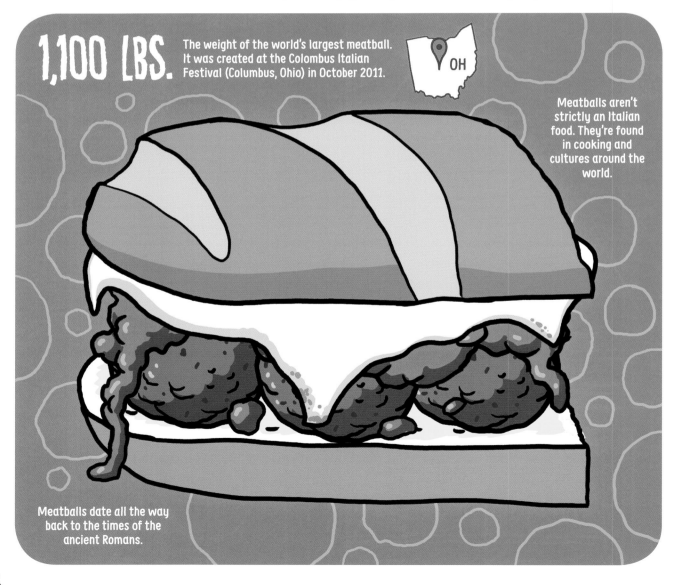

1,100 LBS. The weight of the world's largest meatball. It was created at the Colombus Italian Festival (Columbus, Ohio) in October 2011.

OH

Meatballs aren't strictly an Italian food. They're found in cooking and cultures around the world.

Meatballs date all the way back to the times of the ancient Romans.

HOAGIE ROLL

MOZZARELLA CHEESE

MARINARA SAUCE

MEATBALLS

HOAGIE ROLL

You can make meatball sliders using the same fillings with smaller rolls/buns.

Add parmesan to make your sub extra cheesy!

No leftovers? No problem! Frozen meatballs work just as well as leftovers.

CUSTOMIZE IT!

Meatballs are often made with a mixture of ground beef, pork, or sausage, but you can just as easily use ground turkey or chicken instead (poultry makes meatballs even more moist!).

Once you've assembled your sammie (minus the top), a few minutes under the broiler in the oven will do the trick!

TIMER 2:50 | BROIL | HI

Try it with

SIDE SALAD

COLA

HAM AND PINEAPPLE

Ham and pineapple aren't just pizza toppings anymore — this Hawaiian-inspired combo is also scrumptious on a sandwich! The sweet juice of pineapple perfectly complements the savory taste of ham, and you can never go wrong when you add cheese to the mix. With a grownup's help, grill the whole thing up until the bread is golden, the cheese is melty, and the ham is hot, and then dig in!

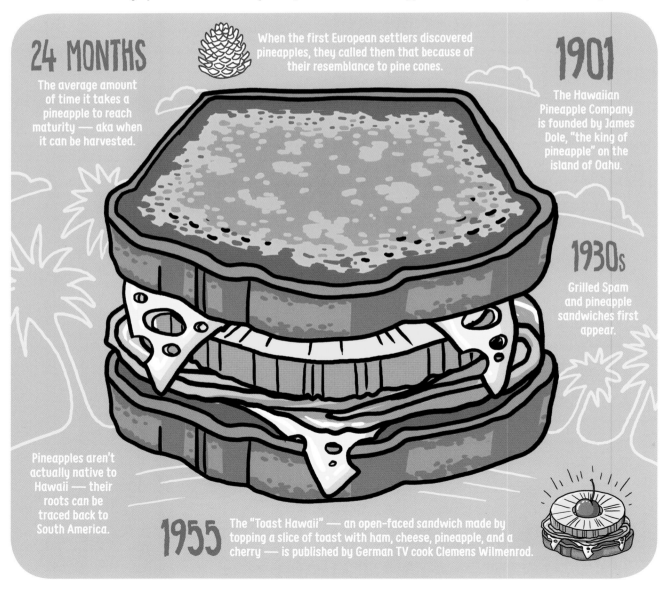

24 MONTHS
The average amount of time it takes a pineapple to reach maturity — aka when it can be harvested.

When the first European settlers discovered pineapples, they called them that because of their resemblance to pine cones.

1901
The Hawaiian Pineapple Company is founded by James Dole, "the king of pineapple" on the island of Oahu.

1930s
Grilled Spam and pineapple sandwiches first appear.

Pineapples aren't actually native to Hawaii — their roots can be traced back to South America.

1955
The "Toast Hawaii" — an open-faced sandwich made by topping a slice of toast with ham, cheese, pineapple, and a cherry — is published by German TV cook Clemens Wilmenrod.

WHEAT BREAD

Don't forget to butter the outside of both slices of bread before grilling!

SWISS CHEESE

Swap out the Swiss for mozzarella, add tomato sauce, and make your ham and pineapple a modified pizza sandwich!

PINEAPPLE

Fresh or canned pineapple both work — use whatever you have on hand!

HAM

SWISS CHEESE

WHEAT BREAD

Grill your sandwich for a couple minutes on each side, until the bread is golden-brown and the cheese is melted.

If you have a panini press you can use that in place of a skillet or grill pan.

PIZZA MELT

What's better than pizza? Trick question — nothing is better than pizza! Well, unless you count this pizza sandwich, that is. A culinary masterpiece that combines the best of both worlds — pizza and sandwiches — this ooey, gooey, cheesy creation can be personalized any way you like. Our version includes the classic combo of pepperoni and mozzarella, but feel free to substitute another meat, or opt for veggies to lighten up your sandwich a bit. Just don't skimp on the cheese!

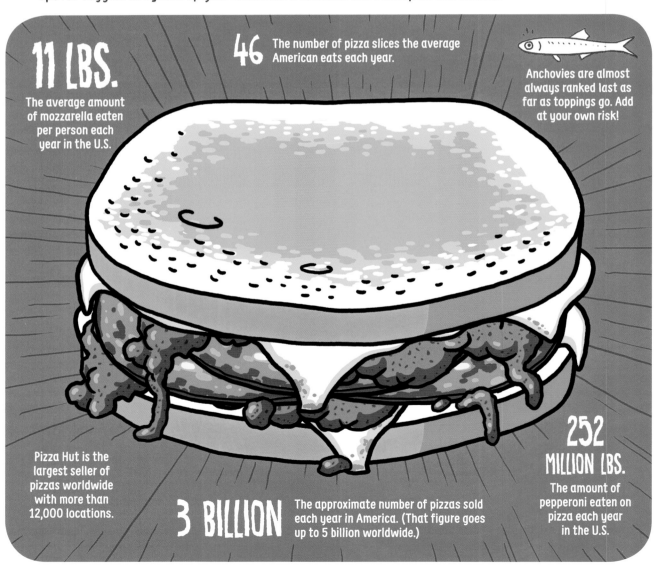

11 LBS.
The average amount of mozzarella eaten per person each year in the U.S.

46 The number of pizza slices the average American eats each year.

Anchovies are almost always ranked last as far as toppings go. Add at your own risk!

Pizza Hut is the largest seller of pizzas worldwide with more than 12,000 locations.

3 BILLION The approximate number of pizzas sold each year in America. (That figure goes up to 5 billion worldwide.)

252 MILLION LBS.
The amount of pepperoni eaten on pizza each year in the U.S.

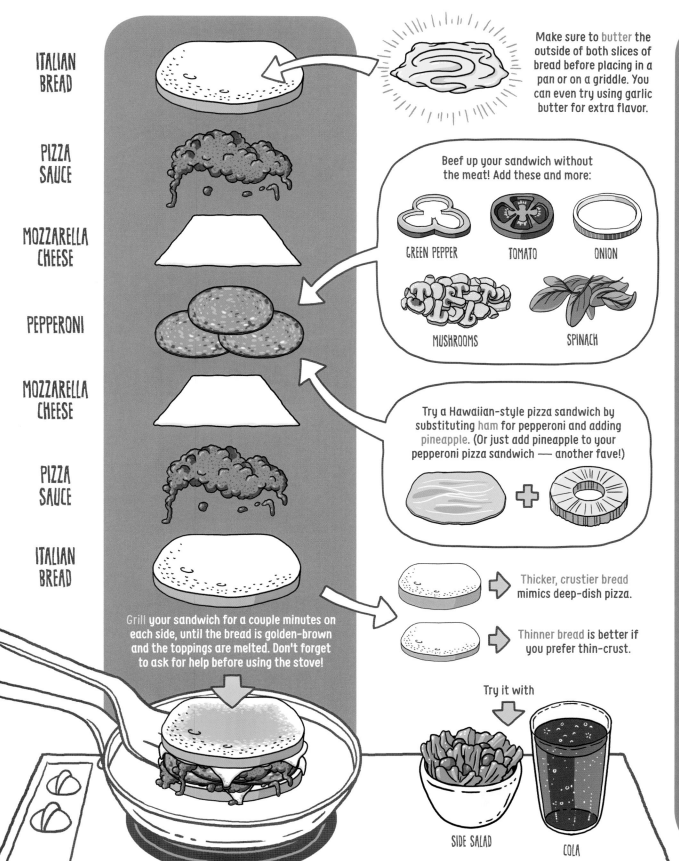

ITALIAN BREAD

PIZZA SAUCE

MOZZARELLA CHEESE

PEPPERONI

MOZZARELLA CHEESE

PIZZA SAUCE

ITALIAN BREAD

Make sure to butter the outside of both slices of bread before placing in a pan or on a griddle. You can even try using garlic butter for extra flavor.

Beef up your sandwich without the meat! Add these and more:

GREEN PEPPER   TOMATO   ONION

MUSHROOMS   SPINACH

Try a Hawaiian-style pizza sandwich by substituting ham for pepperoni and adding pineapple. (Or just add pineapple to your pepperoni pizza sandwich — another fave!)

Grill your sandwich for a couple minutes on each side, until the bread is golden-brown and the toppings are melted. Don't forget to ask for help before using the stove!

Thicker, crustier bread mimics deep-dish pizza.

Thinner bread is better if you prefer thin-crust.

Try it with

SIDE SALAD   COLA

MONTE CRISTO

A traditional Monte Cristo sandwich is fried as a whole, but let's face it — that sounds like a mess. And who needs to bust out the fryer when you have leftovers? This easy-to-make Monte Cristo features leftover French toast, offering the perfect sweet touch to balance savory ham, turkey, and Swiss. With a grownup's help, heat the sandwich in a pan or on a griddle to melt the cheese and reheat the French toast. Don't forget to dust the whole thing with powdered sugar before digging in.

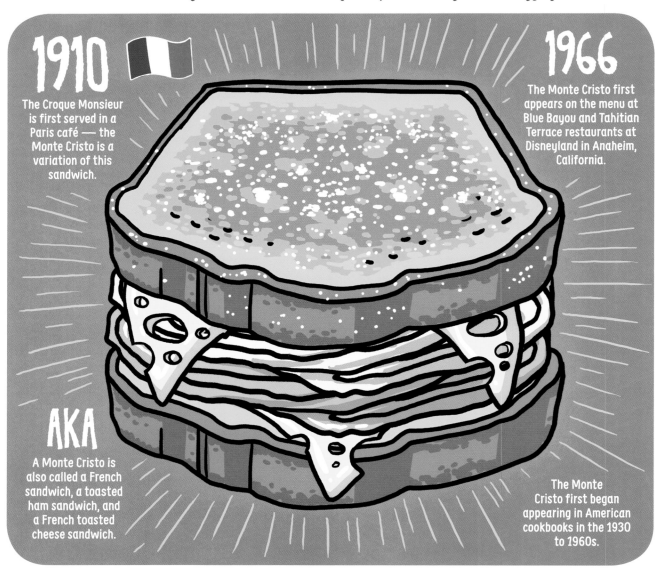

1910

The Croque Monsieur is first served in a Paris café — the Monte Cristo is a variation of this sandwich.

1966

The Monte Cristo first appears on the menu at Blue Bayou and Tahitian Terrace restaurants at Disneyland in Anaheim, California.

AKA

A Monte Cristo is also called a French sandwich, a toasted ham sandwich, and a French toasted cheese sandwich.

The Monte Cristo first began appearing in American cookbooks in the 1930 to 1960s.

FRENCH TOAST

SWISS CHEESE

TURKEY

HAM

SWISS CHEESE

FRENCH TOAST

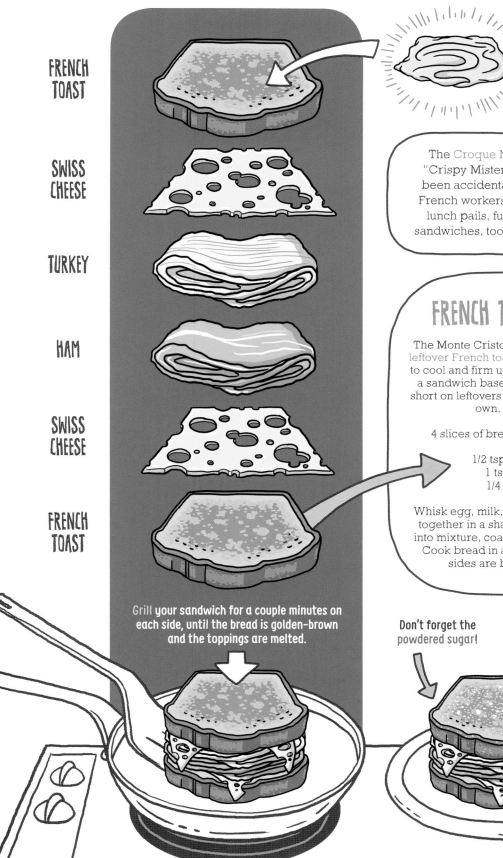

Don't forget to butter the outside of your bread before grilling!

The Croque Monsieur, French for "Crispy Mister," is rumored to have been accidentally created when two French workers accidentally left their lunch pails, full of ham and cheese sandwiches, too close to a hot radiator.

FRENCH TOAST RECIPE

The Monte Cristo is easy to make using leftover French toast. The bread has time to cool and firm up before being used as a sandwich base. But if you're running short on leftovers and want to make your own, it's simple!

4 slices of bread (day old is best)
1 egg
1/2 tsp. cinnamon
1 tsp. vanilla
1/4 cup milk

Whisk egg, milk, vanilla, and cinnamon together in a shallow bowl. Dip bread into mixture, coating both sides evenly. Cook bread in a hot skillet until both sides are browned. Enjoy!

Grill your sandwich for a couple minutes on each side, until the bread is golden-brown and the toppings are melted.

Don't forget the powdered sugar!

Try your Monte Cristo with a side of sweet jam for dipping!

MONTE CRISTO

REUBEN

The origin of the Reuben sandwich involves a tale of two Reubens — Arnold Reuben, owner of Reuben's Restaurant and Delicatessen in New York City, and Reuben Kulakofsky, a member of a weekly poker group at the Blackstone Hotel in Omaha, Nebraska. Both men have been credited with creating the first Reuben sandwich. Whoever was behind the original, this combination of corned beef, Swiss cheese, sauerkraut, and Russian dressing piled high between two slices of rye bread is a classic.

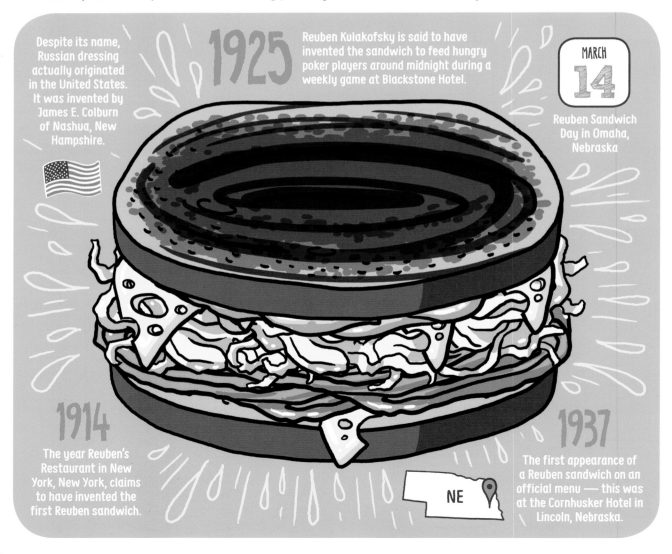

Despite its name, Russian dressing actually originated in the United States. It was invented by James E. Colburn of Nashua, New Hampshire.

1925

Reuben Kulakofsky is said to have invented the sandwich to feed hungry poker players around midnight during a weekly game at Blackstone Hotel.

MARCH
14

Reuben Sandwich Day in Omaha, Nebraska

1914

The year Reuben's Restaurant in New York, New York, claims to have invented the first Reuben sandwich.

NE

1937

The first appearance of a Reuben sandwich on an official menu — this was at the Cornhusker Hotel in Lincoln, Nebraska.

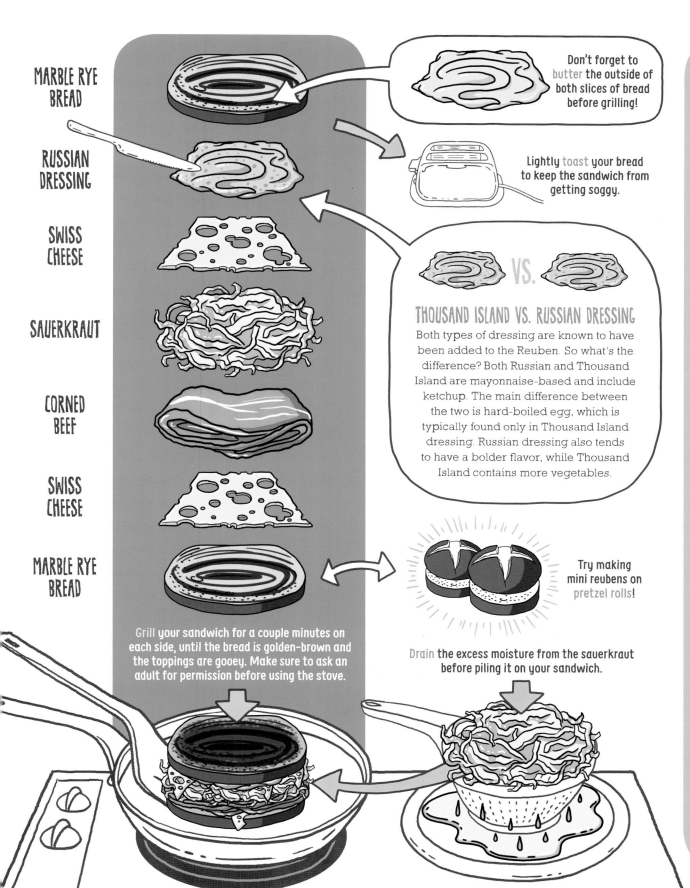

MARBLE RYE BREAD

RUSSIAN DRESSING

SWISS CHEESE

SAUERKRAUT

CORNED BEEF

SWISS CHEESE

MARBLE RYE BREAD

Don't forget to butter the outside of both slices of bread before grilling!

Lightly toast your bread to keep the sandwich from getting soggy.

VS.

THOUSAND ISLAND VS. RUSSIAN DRESSING

Both types of dressing are known to have been added to the Reuben. So what's the difference? Both Russian and Thousand Island are mayonnaise-based and include ketchup. The main difference between the two is hard-boiled egg, which is typically found only in Thousand Island dressing. Russian dressing also tends to have a bolder flavor, while Thousand Island contains more vegetables.

Try making mini reubens on pretzel rolls!

Grill your sandwich for a couple minutes on each side, until the bread is golden-brown and the toppings are gooey. Make sure to ask an adult for permission before using the stove.

Drain the excess moisture from the sauerkraut before piling it on your sandwich.

REUBEN

VERMONTER

A local favorite out of Burlington, Vermont, the Vermonter is a sandwich that's all about the local ingredients, namely delicious sharp Vermont white cheddar. This sweet-and-savory sammie also features an irresistible combination of ham, turkey, tart green apples, and honey mustard, all grilled together between thick cinnamon raisin bread. Don't forget to ask a grownup for help before grilling!

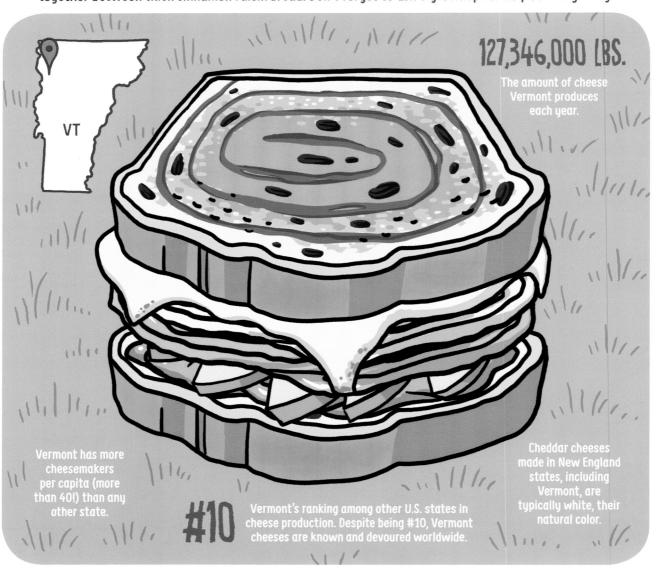

VT

127,346,000 LBS.
The amount of cheese Vermont produces each year.

Vermont has more cheesemakers per capita (more than 40!) than any other state.

#10
Vermont's ranking among other U.S. states in cheese production. Despite being #10, Vermont cheeses are known and devoured worldwide.

Cheddar cheeses made in New England states, including Vermont, are typically white, their natural color.

CINNAMON RAISIN BREAD

WHITE CHEDDAR CHEESE

TURKEY

HAM

GREEN APPLE

HONEY MUSTARD

CINNAMON RAISIN BREAD

Don't forget to butter the outside of both slices of bread before grilling!

OR: Try using apple butter (in place of regular butter) on the outside of your sandwich before grilling for an extra-sweet treat.

Grill your sandwich for a couple minutes on each side, until the bread is golden-brown and the toppings are melty.

1990s

When the Vermonter first originated at Sweetwater's, a popular Burlington restaurant. Cook and waiter Jason Maroney was the man behind the soon-to-be famous sammie.

Serve with another New England classic: salt and vinegar potato chips.

CUBAN

Whether you call it a Cuban, a Cubano, a Cuban mix, or even a mixito, this regional sandwich is instantly recognizable. But where it originated in the U.S. is hotly debated. Both Tampa and Miami, Florida, claim this regional treat as their own. Most historians side with team Tampa. When cigar factories popped up in Key West, Florida, and later moved to the Ybor City neighborhood in Tampa. Restaurants near the factories started serving the Cuban to feed workers, and it became so popular it eventually appeared in other Cuban communities in Florida, including Miami.

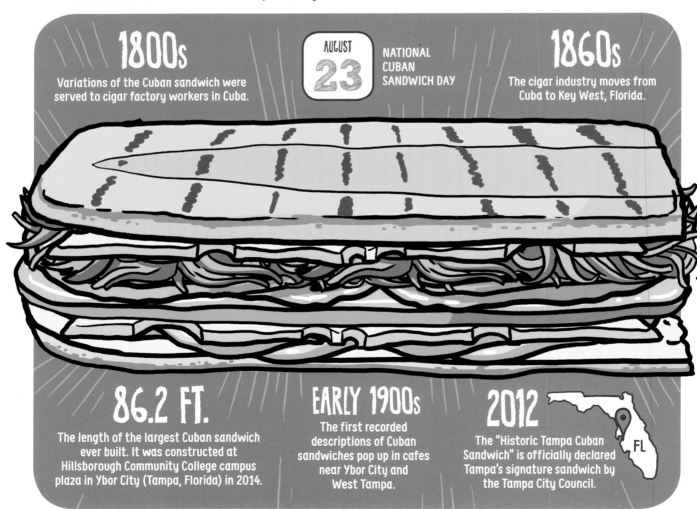

1800s
Variations of the Cuban sandwich were served to cigar factory workers in Cuba.

AUGUST 23
NATIONAL CUBAN SANDWICH DAY

1860s
The cigar industry moves from Cuba to Key West, Florida.

86.2 FT.
The length of the largest Cuban sandwich ever built. It was constructed at Hillsborough Community College campus plaza in Ybor City (Tampa, Florida) in 2014.

EARLY 1900s
The first recorded descriptions of Cuban sandwiches pop up in cafes near Ybor City and West Tampa.

2012
The "Historic Tampa Cuban Sandwich" is officially declared Tampa's signature sandwich by the Tampa City Council.

FL

CUBAN BREAD

A true Cuban sandwich should be 8–12" LONG.

Cuban bread is key to a real Cuban sandwich. It's a long, crusty loaf with a soft interior that's been split down the middle.

SWISS CHEESE

Cuban sandwiches in Tampa, Florida, often contain Genoa salami, a nod to the Italian immigrants who lived alongside Cuban immigrants in Ybor City.

PULLED PORK

Use leftover pulled pork from your family BBQ or your favorite BBQ joint!

HAM

NO MINI PICKLES HERE!
Make sure to use long pickle planks for your Cuban so they run the length of the bread.

DILL PICKLE PLANKS

Yellow mustard is the traditional choice for the Cuban, but feel free to experiment with these options as well:

HOT   HONEY   DIJON

SWISS CHEESE

YELLOW MUSTARD

A *plancha* — or sandwich press — is key to creating an authentic Cuban sandwich.

CUBAN BREAD

CUBAN

FRENCH DIP

A distant cousin of the Italian beef, the French dip is yet another sandwich with hotly debated origins. In fact, despite having "French" in its name, the French dip isn't French at all! The name only refers to the French baguette on which it's served. This uniquely American creation, first created in California, features loads of tender roast beef in the middle, is also served with a side of au jus in which to dip the sandwich.

LOS ANGELES
Birthplace of the French dip.

CA

1908
The year Cole's Pacific Electric Buffet and Phillipe the Original, two Los Angeles restaurants, opened. Both claim to have invented the French dip.

AU JUS
French for "with juice"

1918
The year Phillipe's claims its owner, Philippe Mathieu, invented the French dip.

FRENCH BAGUETTE

Add mayo for extra creaminess.

Or try horseradish for extra zip!

SAUTÉED ONIONS

PRO TIP!

Leftover roast beef finds new life in the French dip — just make sure to slice the meat thinly before piling it on the bread. Don't have leftovers? You can buy cooked roast beef at the grocery store or deli to make it easy.

ROAST BEEF

EASY AU JUS RECIPE

You can buy au jus gravy mix at the store, or try your hand at making your own, as long as you have a grownup's permission!

3 cups beef broth
1 tsp. soy sauce
salt and pepper

Heat beef broth and stir in remaining ingredients, adding salt and pepper to taste. If you like your au jus slightly thicker, whisk a few tbs. of flour to the mixture.

FRENCH BAGUETTE

Serve with a side of au jus for dipping, along with a side of french fries. (French dip, french fries, why not?)

(Make sure to ask an adult for permission before using the stove!)

WESTERN

A Western sandwich, also known as a Denver sandwich, is custom made to be eaten for breakfast. That's because the Western sandwich is literally a Western omelet — scrambled eggs, ham, cheese, onion, and green pepper — sandwiched between two slices of bread. But believe it or not, the Western sandwich actually came *before* the Western omelet!

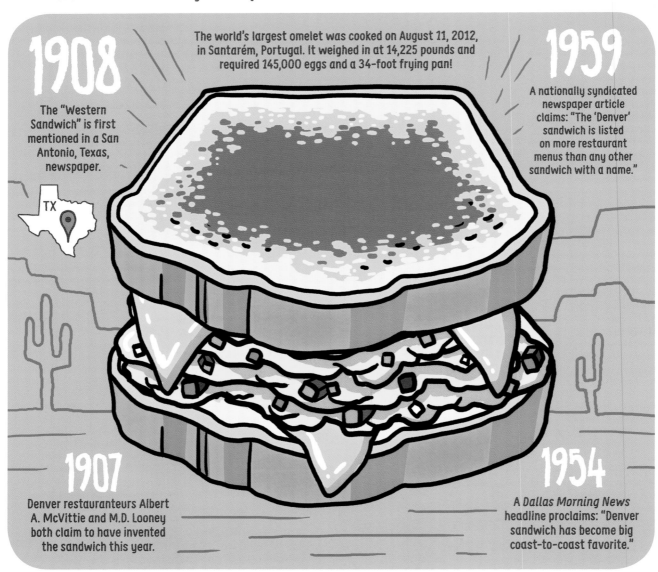

1908

The "Western Sandwich" is first mentioned in a San Antonio, Texas, newspaper.

TX

The world's largest omelet was cooked on August 11, 2012, in Santarém, Portugal. It weighed in at 14,225 pounds and required 145,000 eggs and a 34-foot frying pan!

1959

A nationally syndicated newspaper article claims: "The 'Denver' sandwich is listed on more restaurant menus than any other sandwich with a name."

1907

Denver restauranteurs Albert A. McVittie and M.D. Looney both claim to have invented the sandwich this year.

1954

A *Dallas Morning News* headline proclaims: "Denver sandwich has become big coast-to-coast favorite."

SOURDOUGH TOAST

Make sure to use toasted bread for your sandwich — untoasted won't hold up to your omelet.

AMERICAN CHEESE

DID YOU KNOW?

The Denver omelet might have its roots in the Mile-High City, but the word *omelette* itself is actually French in origin. The spelling we're used to seeing started appearing as far back as the 17th century, but other versions, including *alumelle* and *alumete*, were used as early as 1393.

AMERICAN CHEESE

American cheese is the old standby here, but any cheese will work in this sandwich. Try these for starters:

CHEDDAR   PEPPER JACK

COLBY JACK   PROVOLONE

SOURDOUGH TOAST

FACT:
Oddly enough, finding a Denver sandwich in Denver is virtually impossible!

Serve with hash browns for a real breakfast experience!

WESTERN OMELET

(Make sure to ask an adult for permission before using knives and the stove!)

 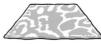

Mix with 2 eggs and a splash of milk.

Salt and pepper to taste.

Pour egg mixture into frying pan and cook on medium heat until set — don't overcook!

 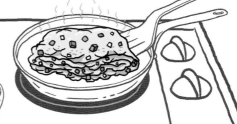

2 slices of ham   1 green pepper   1 small onion   Chop ham, pepper, onion.

CHEESESTEAK

Philadelphia is famous for a number of things, but among sandwich aficionados one thing stands out — the cheesesteak. Often known as a Philadelphia cheesesteak or Philly cheesesteak, this is a sandwich worth making a pilgrimage for. Not ready to head to the East Coast? Never fear! You can whip up this meaty, cheesy delight in your own kitchen. And you should. Because let's face it, almost everything tastes better with cheese, and the same holds true for sandwiches.

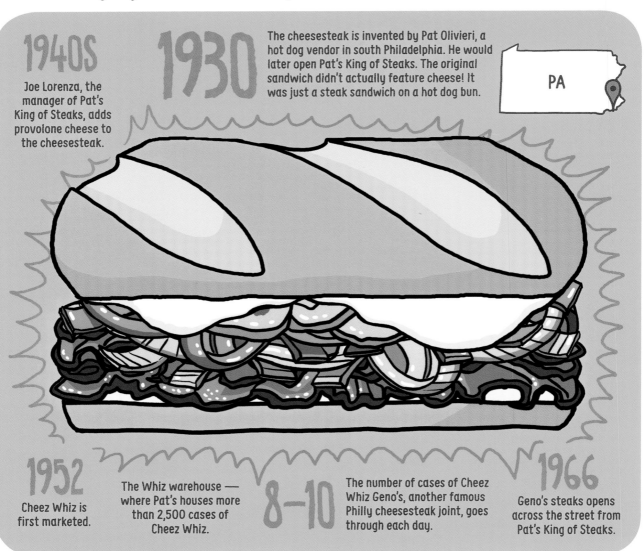

1940S
Joe Lorenza, the manager of Pat's King of Steaks, adds provolone cheese to the cheesesteak.

1930
The cheesesteak is invented by Pat Olivieri, a hot dog vendor in south Philadelphia. He would later open Pat's King of Steaks. The original sandwich didn't actually feature cheese! It was just a steak sandwich on a hot dog bun.

PA

1952
Cheez Whiz is first marketed.

The Whiz warehouse — where Pat's houses more than 2,500 cases of Cheez Whiz.

8–10
The number of cases of Cheez Whiz Geno's, another famous Philly cheesesteak joint, goes through each day.

1966
Geno's steaks opens across the street from Pat's King of Steaks.

FRENCH
BAGUETTE

You don't have to stick with French bread — any long, crusty roll will do. Feeling brave? Switch it up with a round roll, a panini, a wrap, or even an English muffin!

PROVOLONE
CHEESE

VS.

THE GREAT CHEESE DEBATE

The cheesesteak typically comes with one of two types of cheese — provolone or Cheez Whiz. But which is correct is hotly debated. Cheez Whiz offered a quick, easy alternative when it was first introduced, but that wasn't until the 1950s. In fact, the original cheese debate was between American and provolone. Nowadays, Whiz is the favorite for customers at both Pat's and Geno's, the most famous of the Philly cheesesteak joints. But if you ask us, provolone — aka real cheese! — is best. But don't take our word for it. Experiment with your sandwich and try both versions!

SAUTÉED
MUSHROOMS

GRILLED
PEPPERS

GRILLED
ONIONS

STEAK

FRENCH
BAGUETTE

Try a chicken cheesesteak — just substitute grilled chicken for the steak.

(Make sure to ask an adult for permission before using knives and the stove!)

Skirt steak, onion, green peppers, and mushrooms

Chop together to make it easy.

Sauté in pan until meat is cooked through, about 5 minutes.

ITALIAN BEEF

No trip to the Windy City is complete without an Italian beef sandwich. This Chicago staple takes its name from tender, juicy roast beef, shredded or thinly sliced, that's stuffed inside the sammie. The beef is marinated in its own juices and then piled high on a crusty Italian roll. If you have plenty of napkins — or maybe a shower — handy, you can also get the sandwich "wet" — aka soaked in the drippings, bread and all.

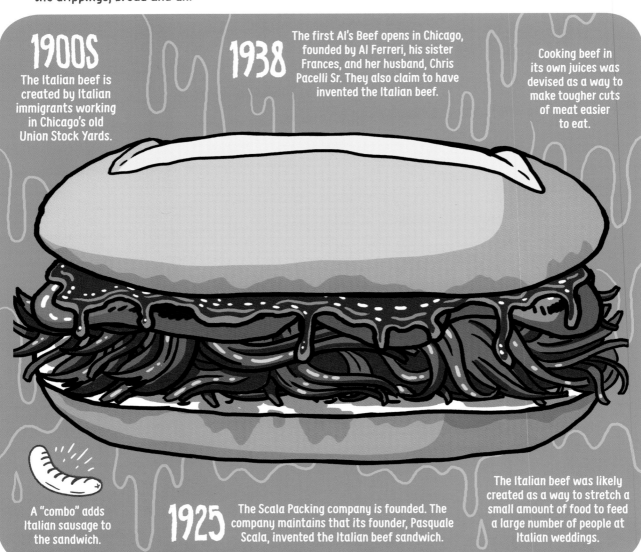

1900S
The Italian beef is created by Italian immigrants working in Chicago's old Union Stock Yards.

1938
The first Al's Beef opens in Chicago, founded by Al Ferreri, his sister Frances, and her husband, Chris Pacelli Sr. They also claim to have invented the Italian beef.

Cooking beef in its own juices was devised as a way to make tougher cuts of meat easier to eat.

A "combo" adds Italian sausage to the sandwich.

1925
The Scala Packing company is founded. The company maintains that its founder, Pasquale Scala, invented the Italian beef sandwich.

The Italian beef was likely created as a way to stretch a small amount of food to feed a large number of people at Italian weddings.

ITALIAN ROLL

BEEF DRIPPINGS

ROASTED PEPPERS

SHREDDED ITALIAN BEEF

ITALIAN ROLL

A "sweet" version (used in this recipe) includes roasted sweet red and green peppers (which you can buy in a jar).

A "hot" beef includes hot giardiniera, an Italian relish with peppers and other vegetables.

Add cheese — provolone or mozzarella are best — and turn your Italian beef into a "cheesy beef" or "cheef."

DRY — the beef is pulled from its juices and allowed to drip mostly dry before being placed on the roll.

WET — the beef is pulled from its juices and immediately put onto a roll; you an also add a spoonful of juice over the top of the meat.

DIPPED — the entire sandwich (including the bread) is dipped in beef juice.

EASY ITALIAN BEEF

(Make sure to ask an adult for permission before using knives and the stove!)

3 lbs. rump roast

1 package Italian salad dressing

1 can (15-oz.) beef broth

8 oz. pepperoncini (plus juice)

Mix all ingredients together in a crockpot, including about half the juice from the pepperoncini. (Use fewer peppers and less juice if you don't like spice.) Turn crockpot on high, and cook for 4–5 hours, until meat is cooked and tender.

Shred your meat and save the liquid. That's your dipping sauce!

ALISON DEERING, AUTHOR

Originally from Michigan — the Mitten State! — Alison learned the value of a good book and a great sandwich early on. After earning a journalism degree from the University of Missouri-Columbia, she started her career as a writer and editor. Alison currently lives in Chicago, Illinois, with her husband, where she makes, eats, and talks about as many sandwiches as humanly possible.

If Alison were a sandwich, she would be a fancy grilled cheese, inspired by the Grilled 3 Cheese at Café Muse in Royal Oak, Michigan.

WHOLE GRAIN BREAD

HAVARTI CHEESE

TOMATO

BASIL

HONEY

FONTINA CHEESE

MOZZARELLA CHEESE

WHOLE GRAIN BREAD

BOB LENTZ, ILLUSTRATOR

Bob is an art director who has designed and illustrated many successful books for children, and is the latter half of the duo Lemke & Lentz, creators of *Book-O-Beards*, part of the Wearable Books series. In his spare time, he likes to talk about food, especially sandwiches. Bob lives in Minnesota, with his wife and children, where they go for long walks, sing old-timey songs, and eat ice cream with too many toppings.

If Bob were a sandwich, he would be "The Snowpig," proudly hailing from Morty's at Hyland Hills Ski Area in Bloomington, Minnesota.

FRENCH BREAD

SRIRACHA

SWEET AND SPICY PICKLES

APPLESAUCE

PROVOLONE CHEESE

PULLED PORK

FRENCH BREAD

READ MORE

Atwood, Lisa. *The Cookbook for Kids: Great Recipes for Kids Who Love to Cook*. San Francisco, Cali.: Weldon Owen, 2016.

Deering, Alison. *Fish and Fowl: Easy and Awesome Sandwiches for Kids*. Between the Bread. Mankato, Minn.: Capstone Press, 2017.

Hoena, Blake and Katrina Jorgensen. *Ballpark Cookbook The American League: Recipes Inspired by Baseball Stadium Foods*. Sports Illustrated Kids. Mankato, Minn.: Capstone Press, 2016.

Use FACTHOUND to find Internet sites related to this book. Just type in 9781515739210 AND GO!